CW01310955

Illustrations Copyright Amy Whitewick, 2016

All rights reserved. No part of this publication may be reproduced, stored in a retrieval system, or transmitted in any form by means electronic, mechanical, photocopying, recording or otherwise, without prior permission of the author.

However, if you wish to photocopy any of the illustrations to colour in for personal use, or show them off as coloured by yourself to your friends on social media, you are free to do so.

#murdermysterycolour

The characters and case in this book are fictional – any resemblance to any persons, living or dead, is purely coincidental.

www.camelotmedia.co.uk

Printed by CreateSpace

THE JANUS INCIDENT

Amy Whitewick

I was called this morning by Sergeant Rowde, who had made a gruesome discovery of the body of a local young girl, mysteriously left in a tree at the edge of a woodland.

I could do with an extra pair of hands to solve this case; you'll do perfectly.

Arm yourself with plenty of colours, and let's get cracking!

Inspector Wolf

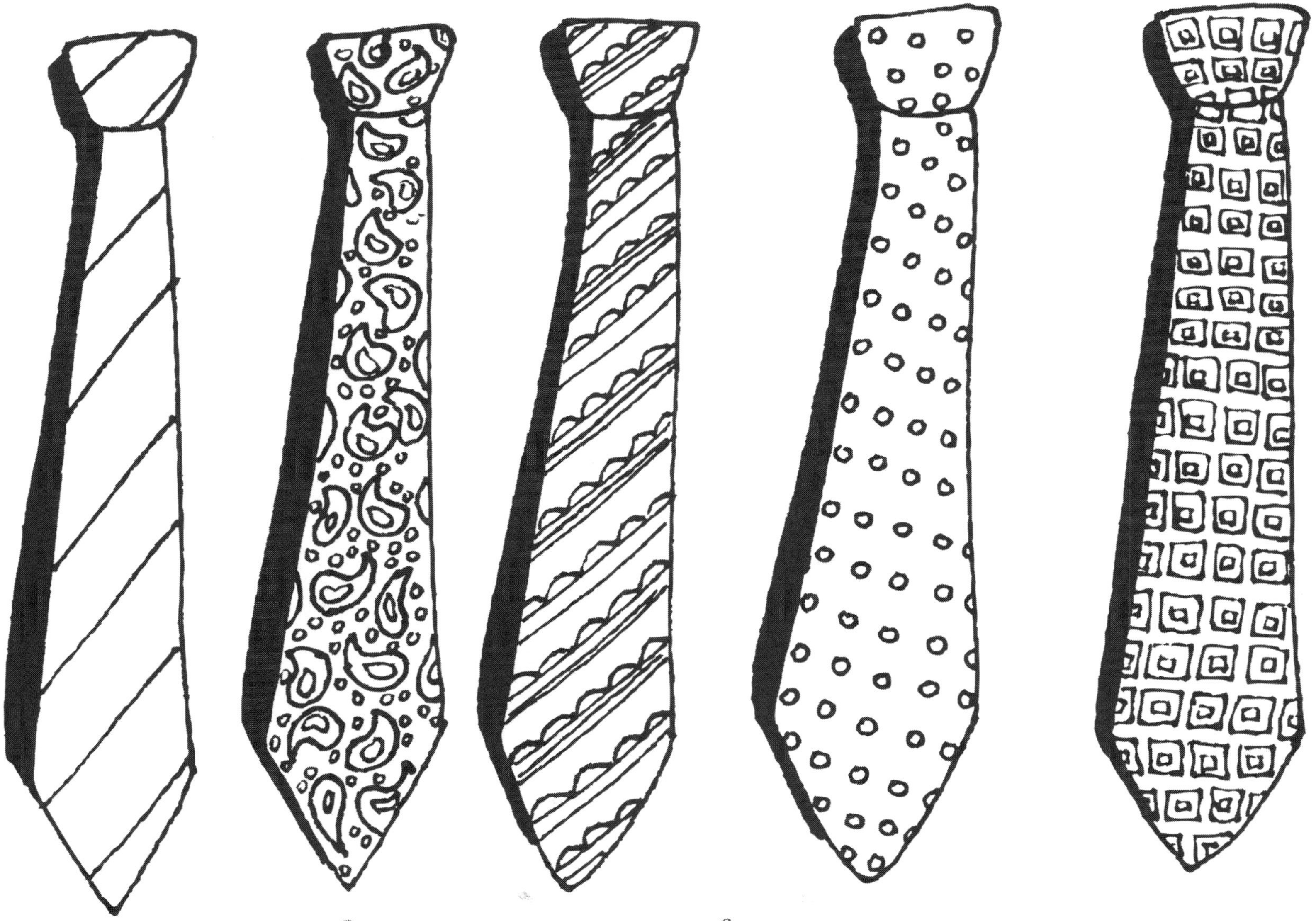

~ Pick me out a nice tie by colouring it in ~

Take care as we approach the scene; it has rained in the past week and the farmer's field is muddy!

The girl appears well dressed, however, her shoes are missing.

The attack seems to be consistent with that of a large animal, with large tears across her upper body. How peculiar.

There are two marks at the base of the trunk. Footprints perhaps?

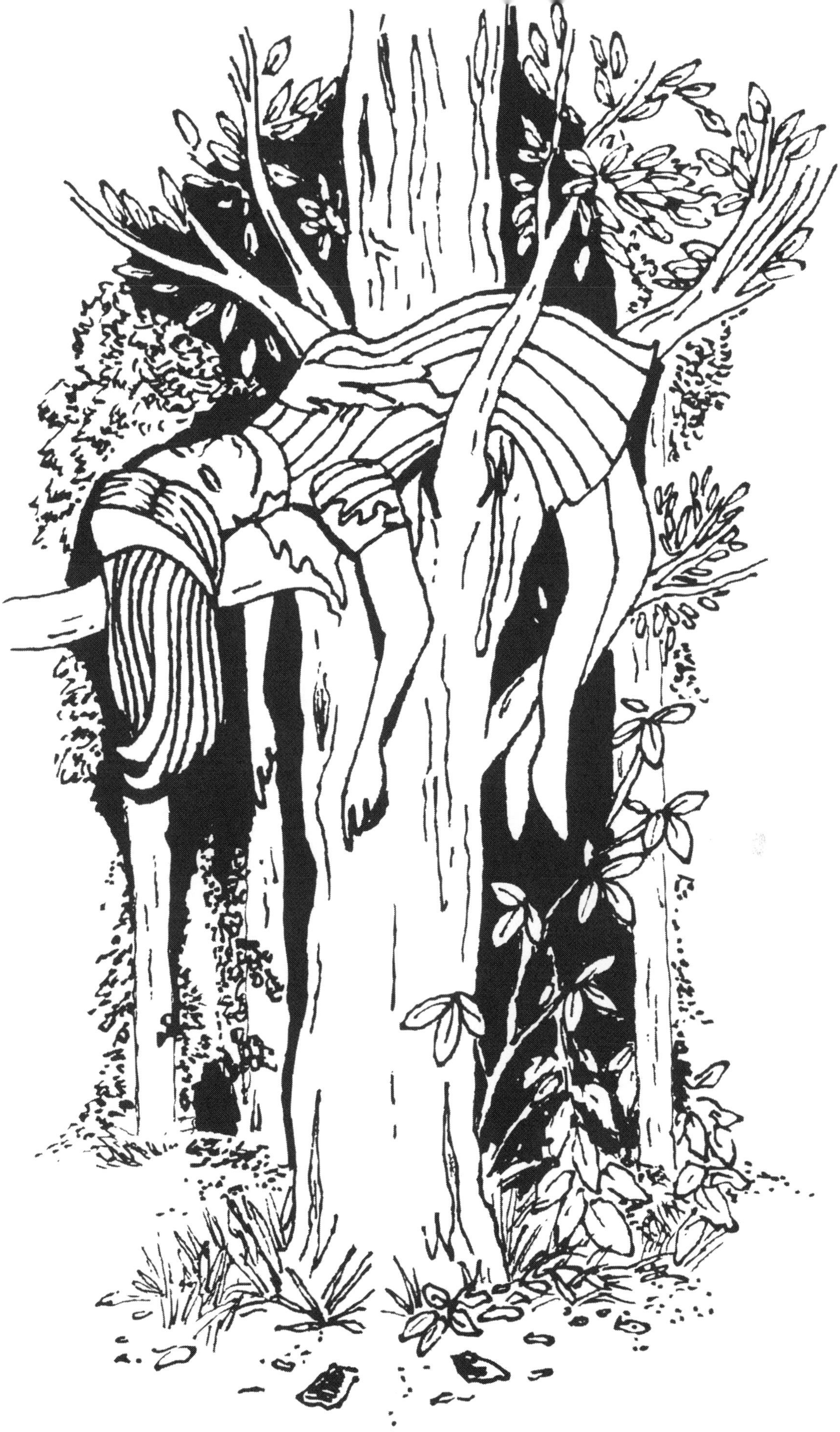

Let's take a look in the victim's handbag which was found dumped in the hedgerow opposite.

The contents are what one might expect in a young ladies personal effects — lipstick, comb, cigarettes.

The torn photo may come in handy — let's keep that one.

The rose is unusual. It could well be a token from a close friend, as it isn't one that can be easily picked from the wild.

~ Find the missing half of the picture and colour it in ~

I recall a painting that hangs in my local public house which depicts the 'Beast of Fingleberry'.

Romantically, many of the locals believe that a leopard escaped from a private collection many years ago and still roams the countryside today.

Leopards hang their prey in trees to avoid unwanted attention from scavengers. It's odd that the girl was found in this manner – perhaps the beast is indeed the culprit.

Surely this would be too easy?

- Find the other two leopards and colour them in -

I've made some calls and contacted the victim's best friend.

When I visited her, she seemed strangely unaffected by the news of her friend's tragedy. She remained hidden behind her dark glasses for the entire interview.

Perhaps she didn't care to show her emotions. Some people can be like that and fear a public display; I know I do.

Her handbag was very similar to her friend's with a smart, chequered pattern.

I showed the woman the torn photo. She explained that her friend tore it in half once she discovered her boyfriend was having an affair.

I asked who her boyfriend was, and she mentioned it was a young man who worked at Janma Seed Company, not far from Fingleberry.

I thanked her and left.

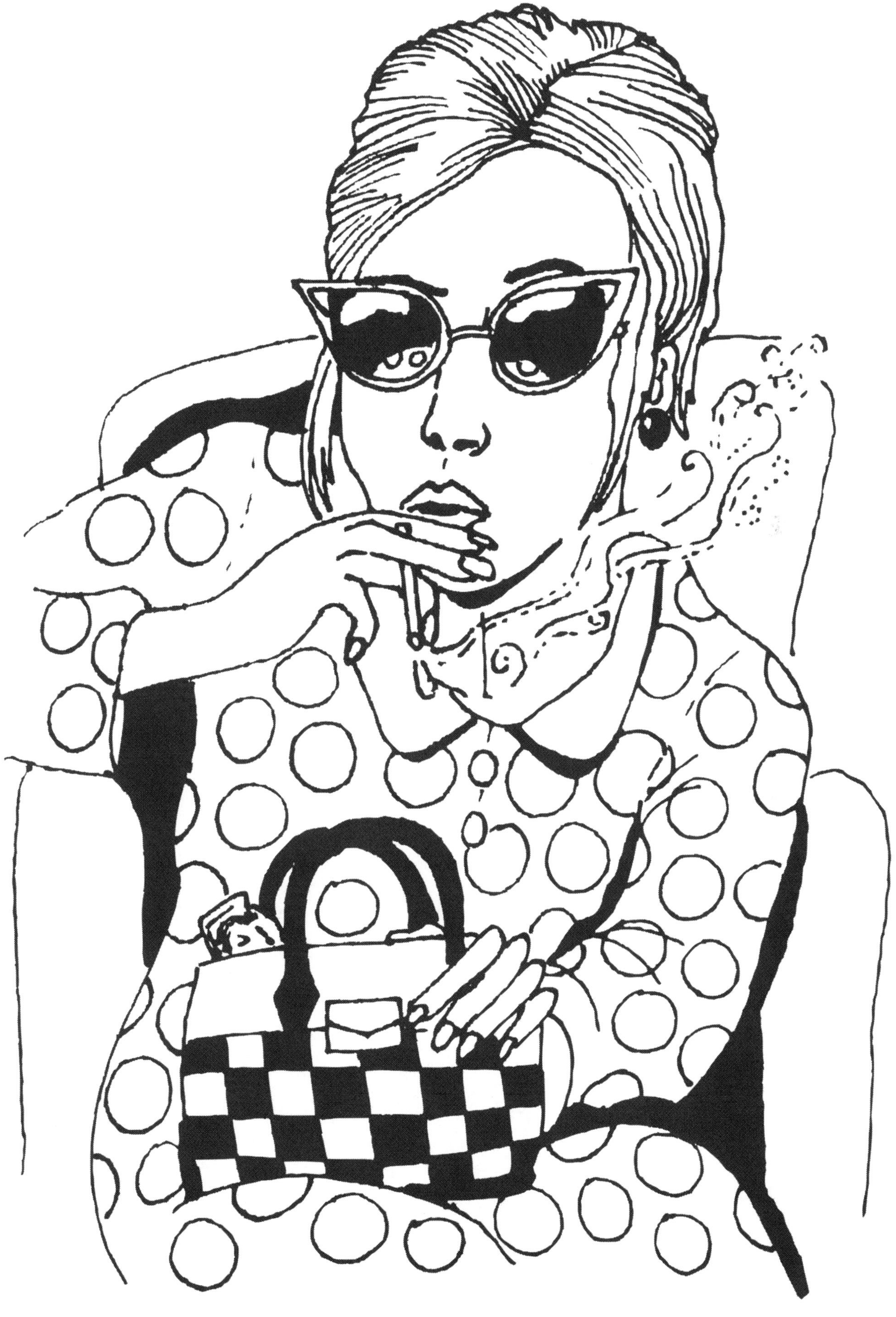

Upon arrival at Janma Seed Company, I found the door unlocked. Although I shouted, no-one came, so I took the opportunity to take a look around.

I spotted a desk with a full cup of tea stood upon it. I dipped my finger in it and discovered it was barely lukewarm, as if it was suddenly left in a hurry.

Various seed labels and notes were left scattered around it. A ring and a jar of powder spilled out nearby.

I scribbled some notes in my book and carried on

- Research the meaning of Digitalis then find and colour them in -

When I approached the conservatory, a young man spotted me and lifted his head in surprise.

His watering can emptied over a cluster of bright red geraniums.

"Who are you?" He asked.

I nodded at him and pulled my identification from my pocket.

I admired the tropical colours of the plants that sprawled in every direction.

"Very nice."

The young man put the can down.

"I'm afraid Mr Redtouch isn't here at the moment. Can I help you?"

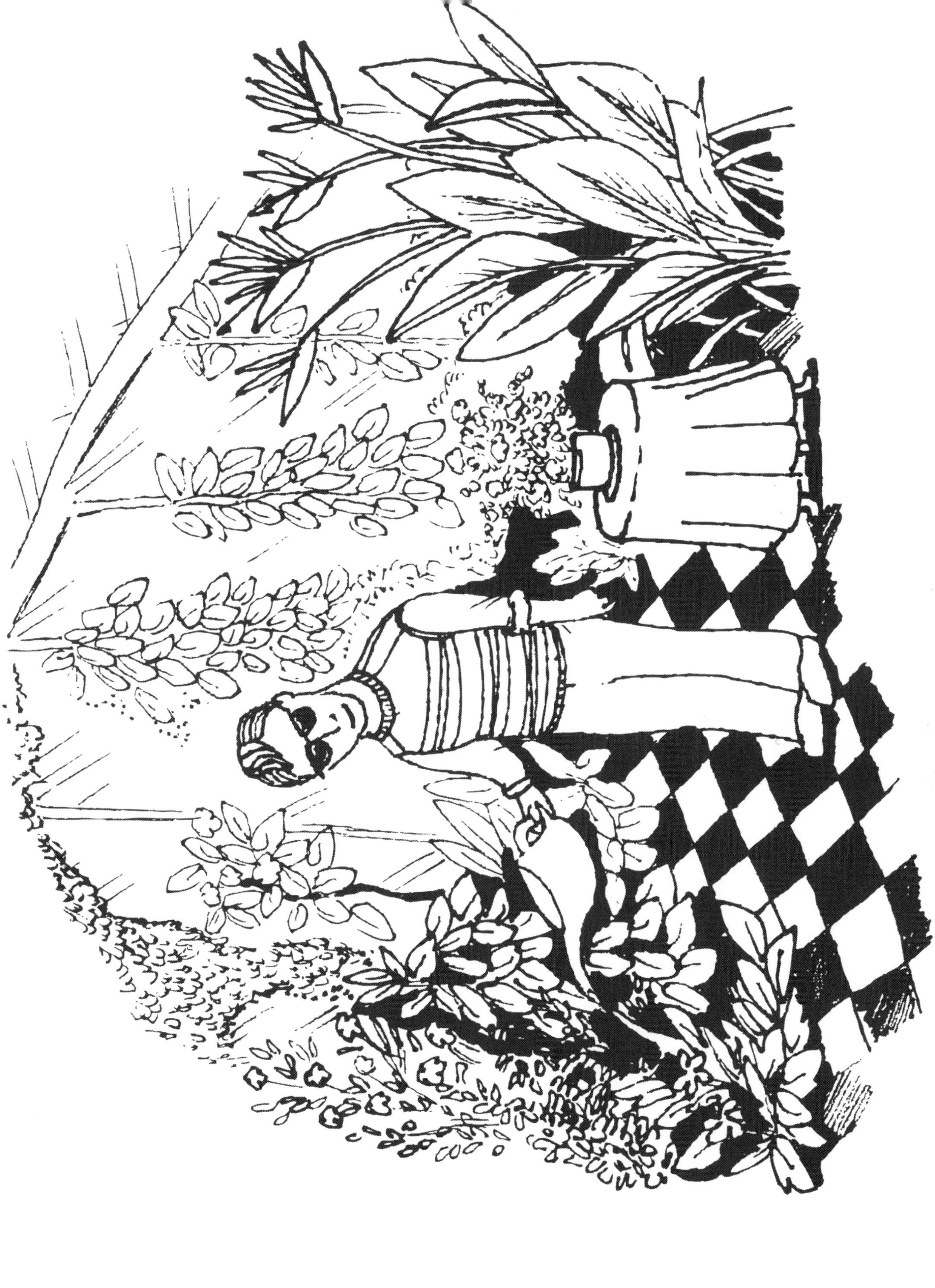

I followed the young man into the garden.

"This is Mr Redtouch's private collection. He has an affinity for poisonous plants and herbs and collects seeds from all around the world."

I looked at a statue of Romulus and Remus nestled amongst some foxgloves.

"Looks as though he has an affinity for Roman history as well."

The young man beckoned me to follow him.

"There's a nice mosaic over here as well."

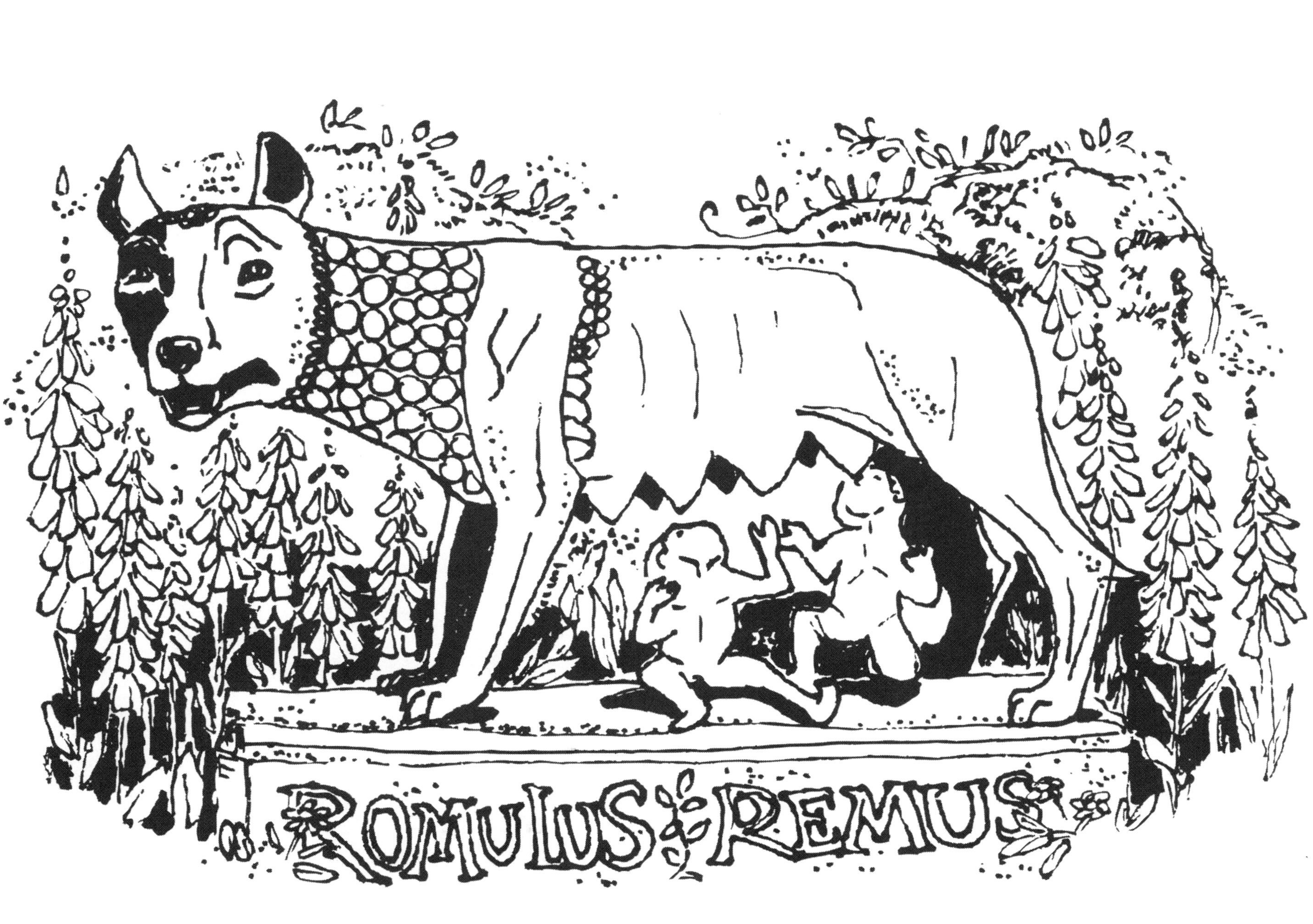
ROMULUS & REMUS

I looked down at the neatly arranged tiles. They depicted the Roman god, Janus.

"An interesting article, indeed, but it's actually you I came to talk to."

The young man looked up in surprise.

"Me? Why?"

"Your name is Simon, isn't it?"

He shook his head.

"Simon isn't here today."

- Find the other Janus head and colour it in -

I followed him over to a set of chairs in front of a large, tropical bush.

"Simon is a temp here."

I opened my notepad.

"Do you know where he lives?"

He shook his head, slightly irritated.

"I don't know, as I said, he's only temporary and no-one knows much about him."

"Did you know that his ex-girlfriend has been murdered?"

His eyebrows twitched slightly behind his dark glasses, but his face remained straight.

"How terrible. I'm sorry to hear that."

He stood upwards.

"If you don't need to ask me anything else, I must get back to work. The plants don't water themselves."

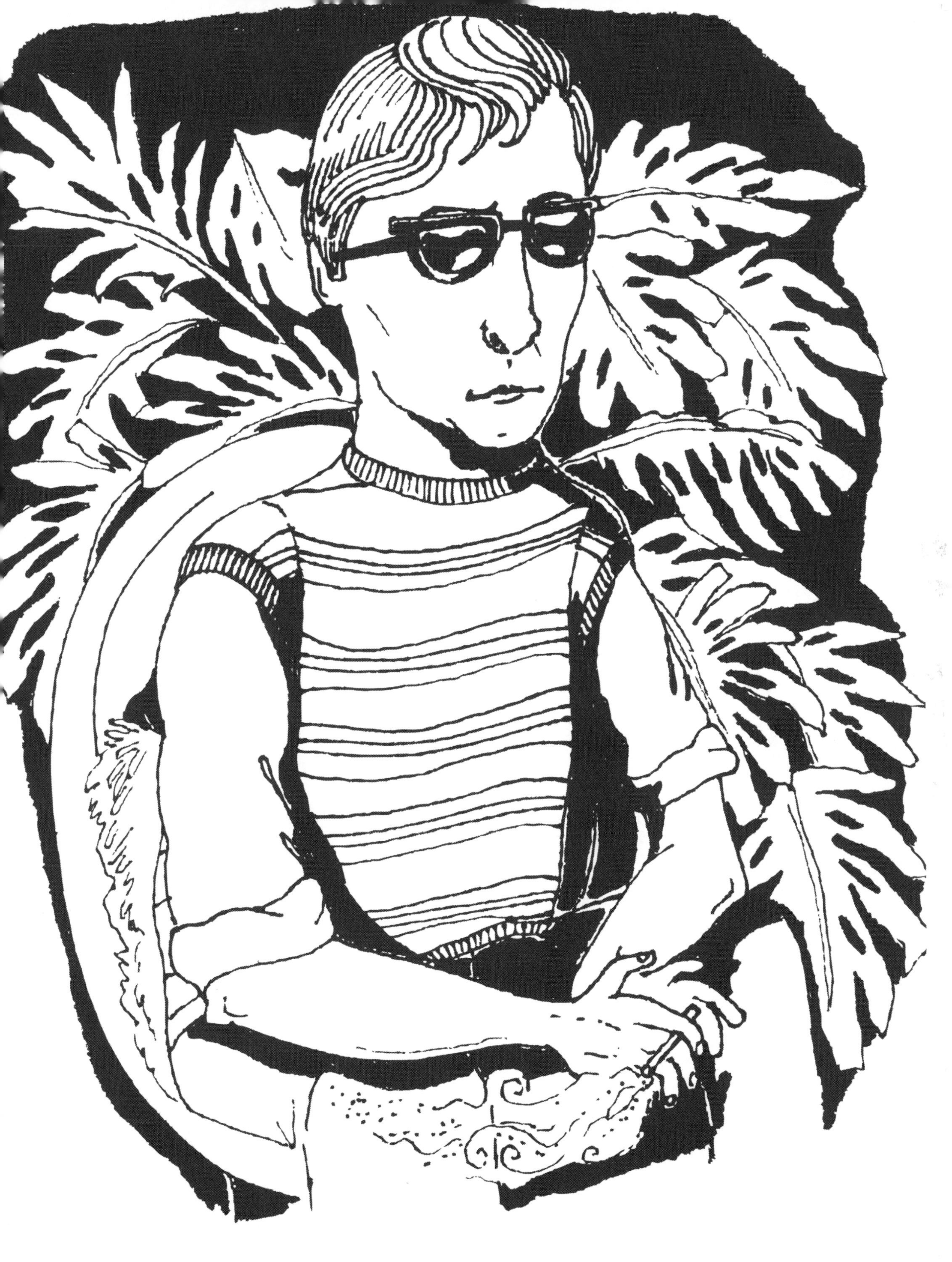

I followed him back through the house and glanced down at another desk which was littered with seed packets.

The young man looked back at me.

"Rare seeds we offer to our best customers. You can have a couple of packets if you like."

I smiled at him and picked out some from the pile and folded them into my pocket.

"Be careful not to spill them into food, they're very poisonous."

- *Find the other five seed packets and colour them in -*

Jars of flowers lined the windowsills of the house.

I spotted a rose that I recognised from the victim's handbag. I stopped and touched the petals gently.

"Could you tell me where this came from?"

The man paused.

"Well, we grow lots of roses here – that one's an unusual variety that we crossed especially to give it the rich colour. Do you like it?"

"Not particularly. I'm not fond of roses."

I followed the young man down the narrow hallway to the door.

Helleborus Foetidus

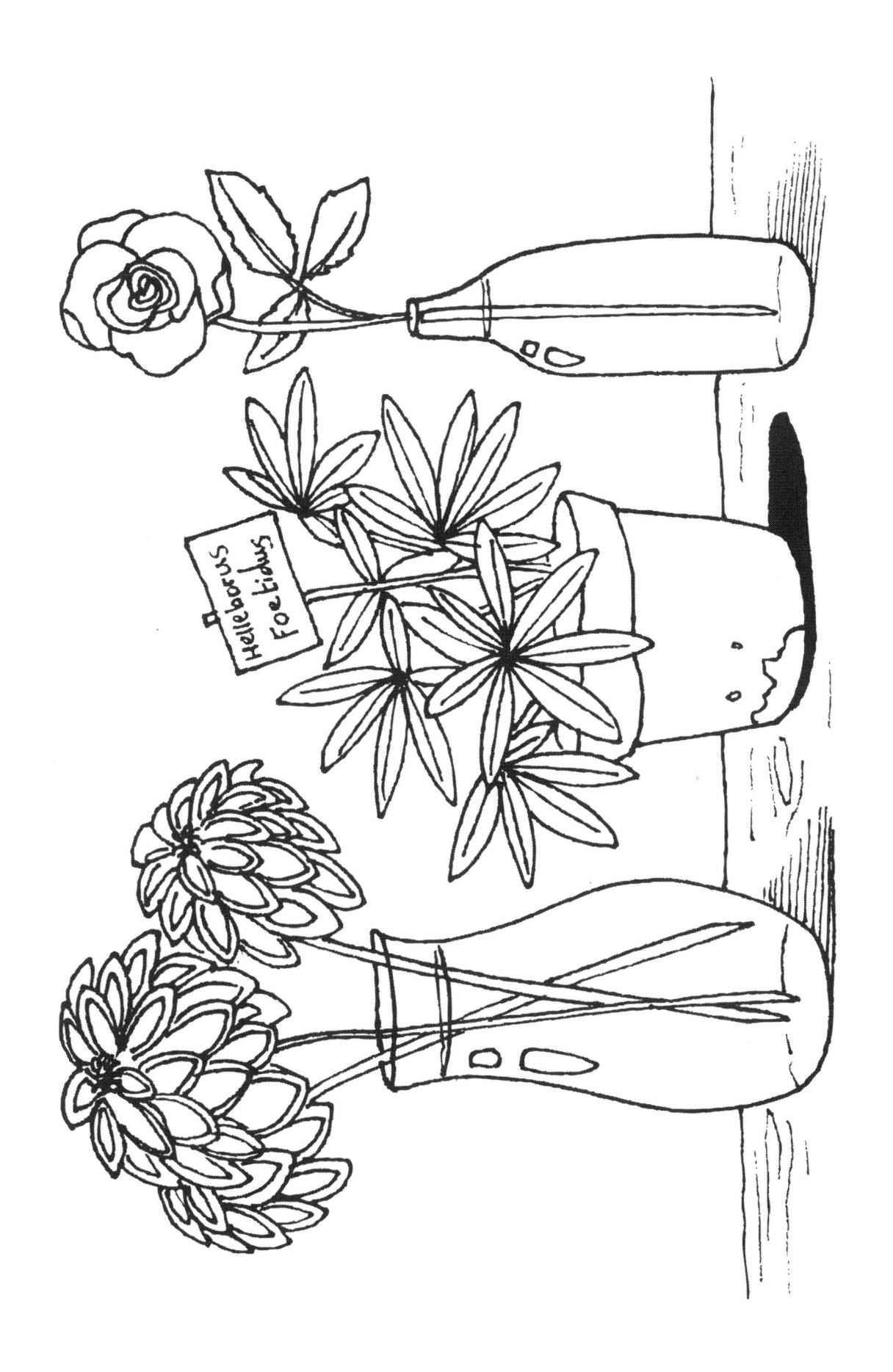

On the wall was a photo of a man next to his son.

"Is that Mr Redtouch?" I asked.

"Yes. That's his son, Graham. Real tragedy that was. He was killed in a horse riding accident."

"Nice car."

The young man paused.

"Sorry?"

I pointed at a picture lower down.

"Oh, yes, Mr Redtouch is fond of his cars."

"Must be a very lucrative business, growing seeds."

He shrugged and showed me out of the door. I walked over to my car and looked back at the large, grand house.

- Find the missing key -

After seeing the young man, I headed back to my office and sat at my desk with the seed packets and my notes in front of me.

It seemed odd that the boyfriend wasn't at the seed company, and neither was Mr Redtouch.

It was almost as though they had anticipated my arrival and fled, leaving the cup of tea behind.

Strangely, there was only one cup, not two.

I thought about the Roman influence of the garden and rummaged through my bookcase to find some books on the subject.

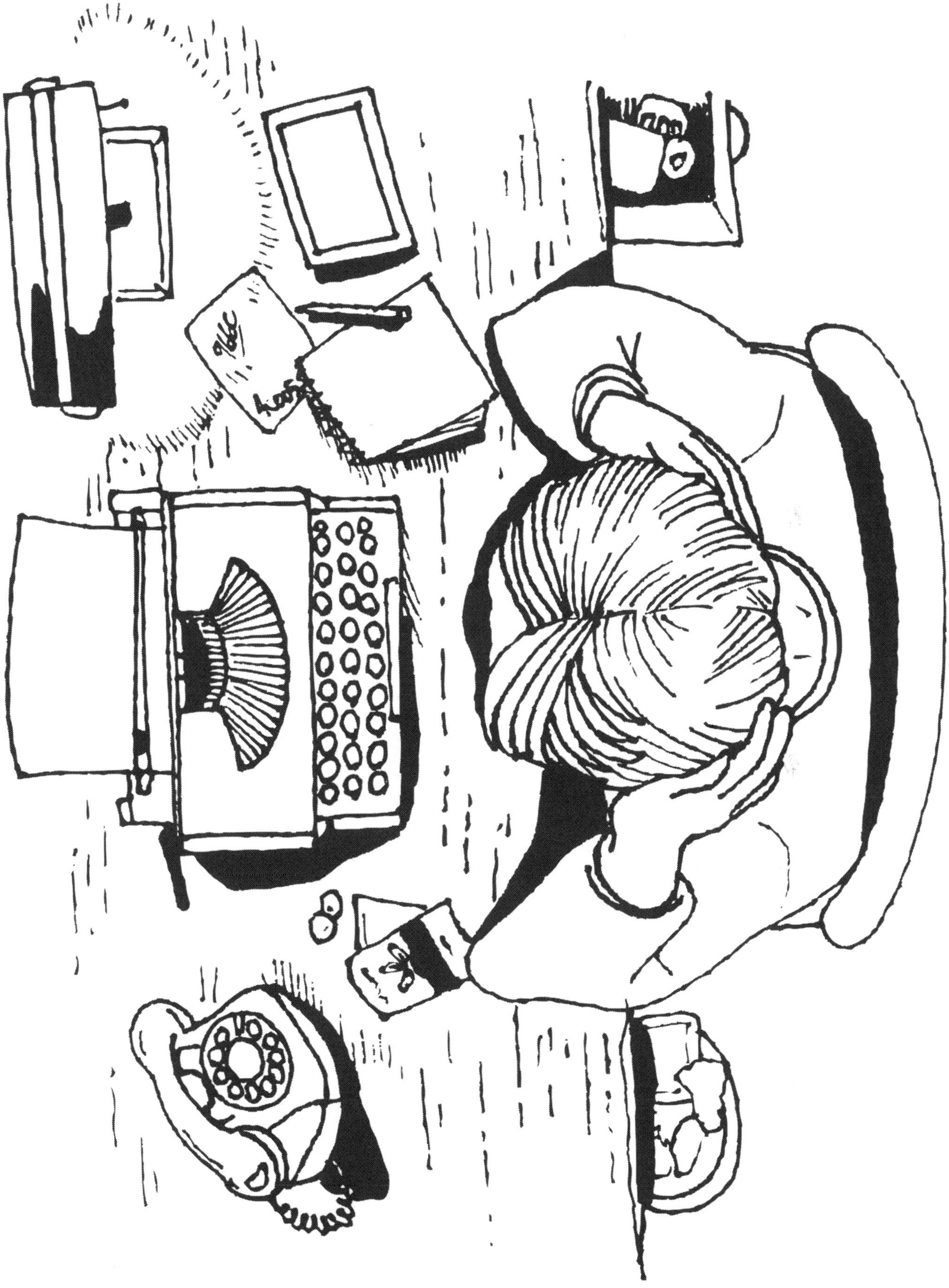

I also pulled out a book on stories of leopards that had escaped from captivity. The tales in there were enough to make anyone think that the slightest wobble of a bush could be dangerous.

I moved on to studying a picture of the Roman god, Janus. The illustration matched the mosaic almost perfectly.

The god was said to be two-headed, a face on the back of a face, hence the term 'two-faced'.

There's certainly something two-sided about this case.

Feeling a mental block coming on, I grabbed my coat and headed for the car.

CASE NO. 35
Matutine Pater
'MORNING FATHER.
Beginning of the day
Janus
ANCIENT ROME
TWO-HEADED GOD
Janma Seed Co.

On the way, my headlights ensnared a fox that turned to look at me as I braked. He looked most annoyed. If foxes had eyebrows, this one had a huge frown as it turned to dash away into the dark.

My heart pounded and my head raced with the thoughts of man eaters.

I shook myself mentally and drove onwards, pulling up in the car park of the appropriately named Fox and Hounds.

A warm and friendly light spilled out from the windows onto the tarmac.

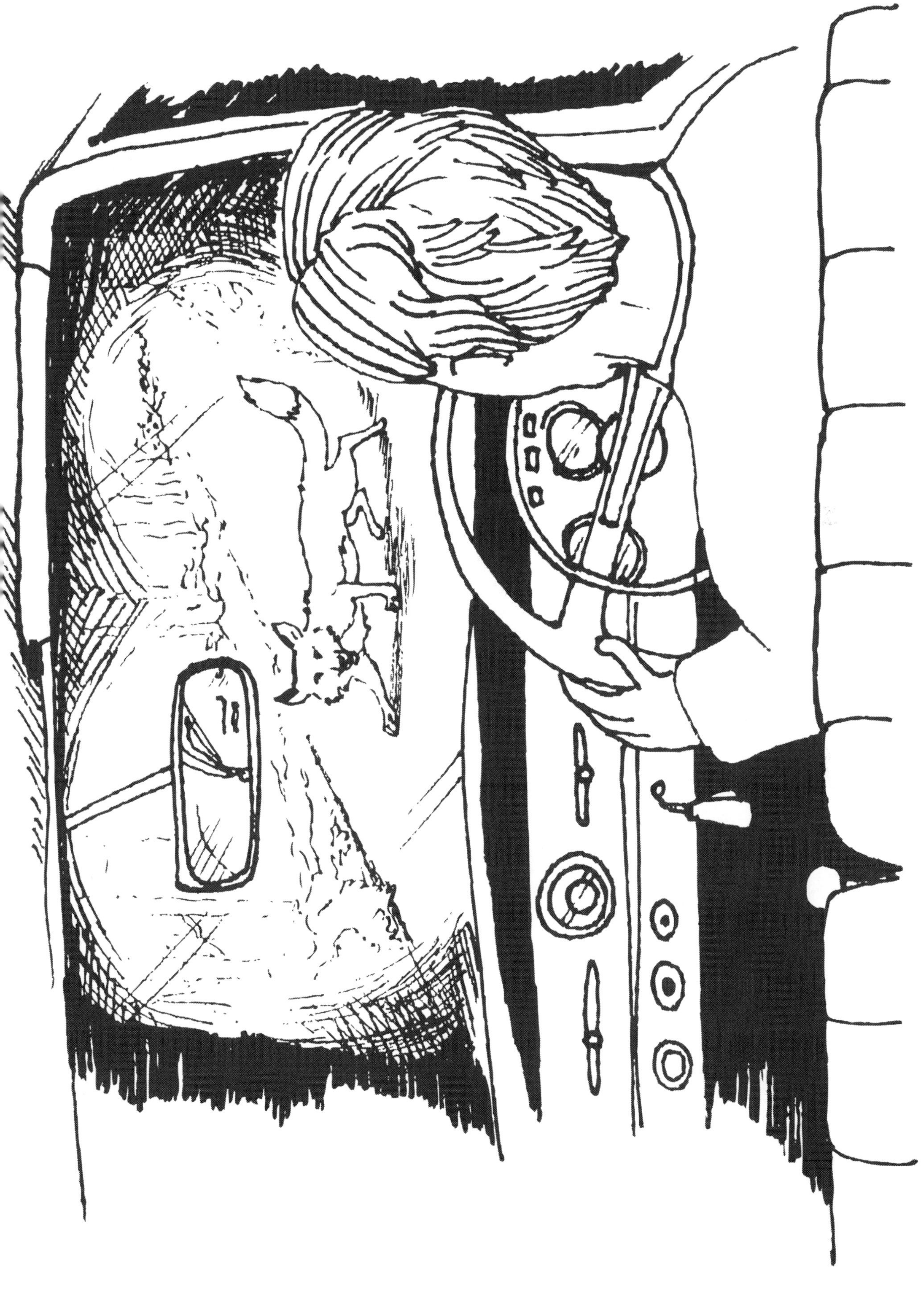

The landlord nodded as I walked in.

It was a quiet evening with very little company, so I perched on one of the bar stools and ordered my usual.

Taking a sip, I overheard a conversation in the corner.

- Give the barstools some pizzazz by drawing some bold patterns on them -

Two of the locals were sat deep in discussion.

Their little terrier sat between them, eyeing up a plate of egg and chips set before his master.

"There's a lovely Hillman been dumped at the edge of the common, you know. Nice colour, too. I wouldn't mind one of them."

The man next to him looked up from his pint.

"'Cor, that sounds good. Has it got those nice red leather seats?"

Before he could answer, I walked up to the men.

"Sorry to interrupt – whereabouts did you see the car?"

They explained its location and I dashed out of the pub.

I heard their faint voices as I crossed the car park.

"He was in a bit of a hurry."

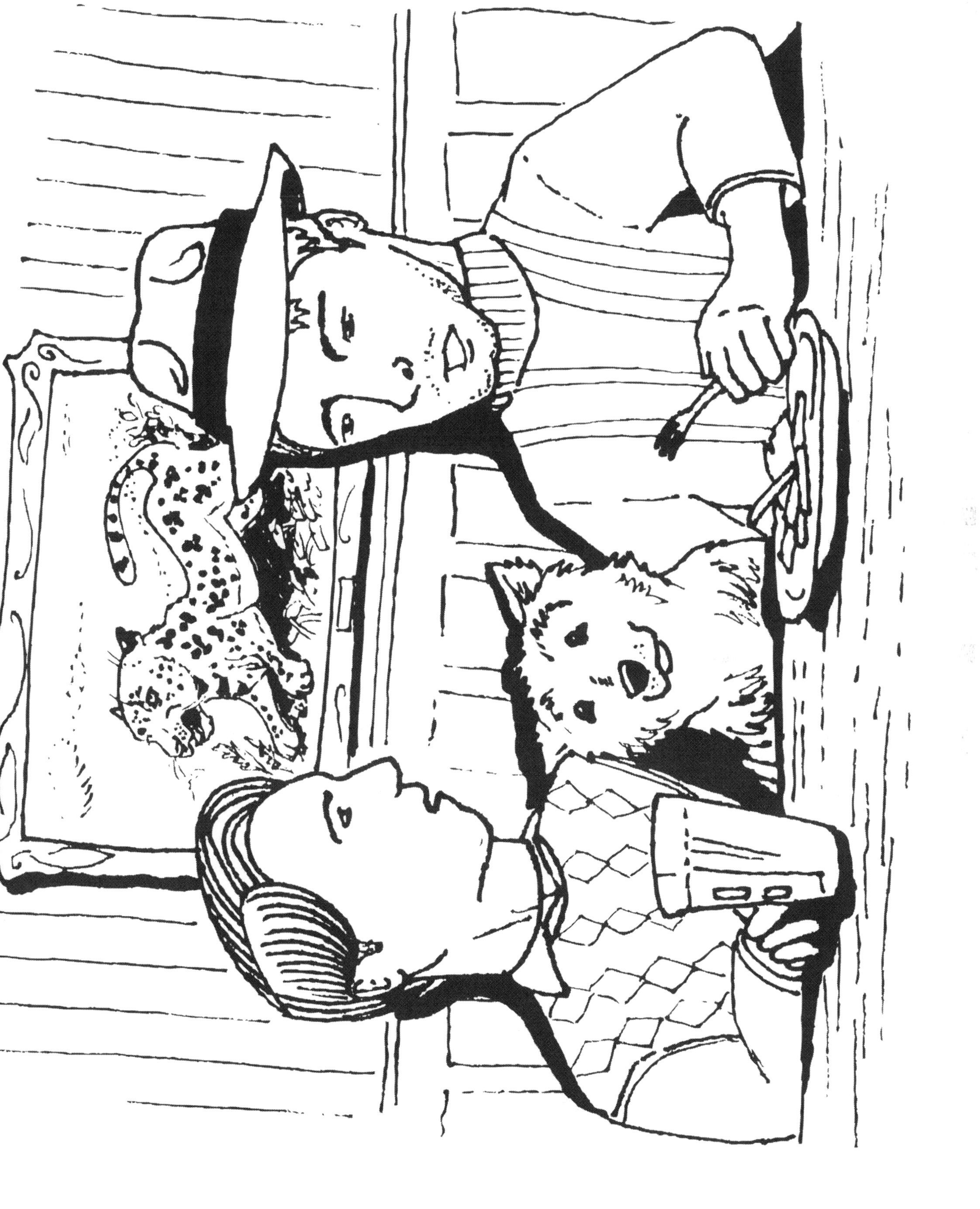

I drove as quickly as I could to the scene and took my torch with me. I wasn't afraid of the dark, but the stories of leopards made me shiver in the cool night air as I made my way over to the vehicle.

Suddenly, I remembered a set of numbers written on a scrap of paper on the desk at the seed company – 966C.

The number plate of the car ended with 966C.

The boot was slightly ajar and I pulled it wide.

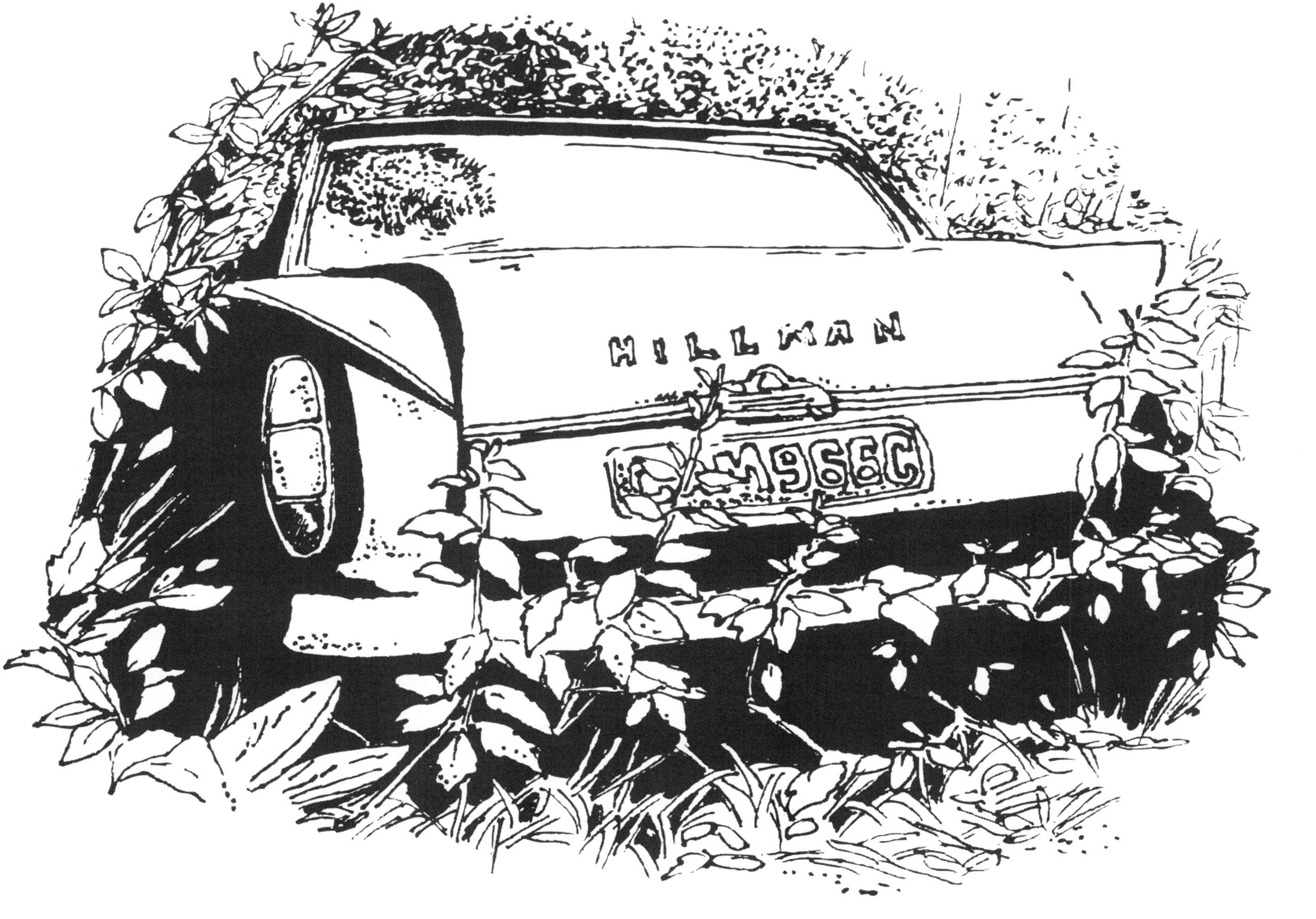
HILLMAN

Grabbing my notepad from my pocket, I scribbled down a quick image of the interior of the boot, which was dirty and stained.

A shoe rested against the back next to a coil of rope.

A boot brush and a soiled blanket covered a knife.

As I bent to take a closer look, I discovered a torn piece of paper.

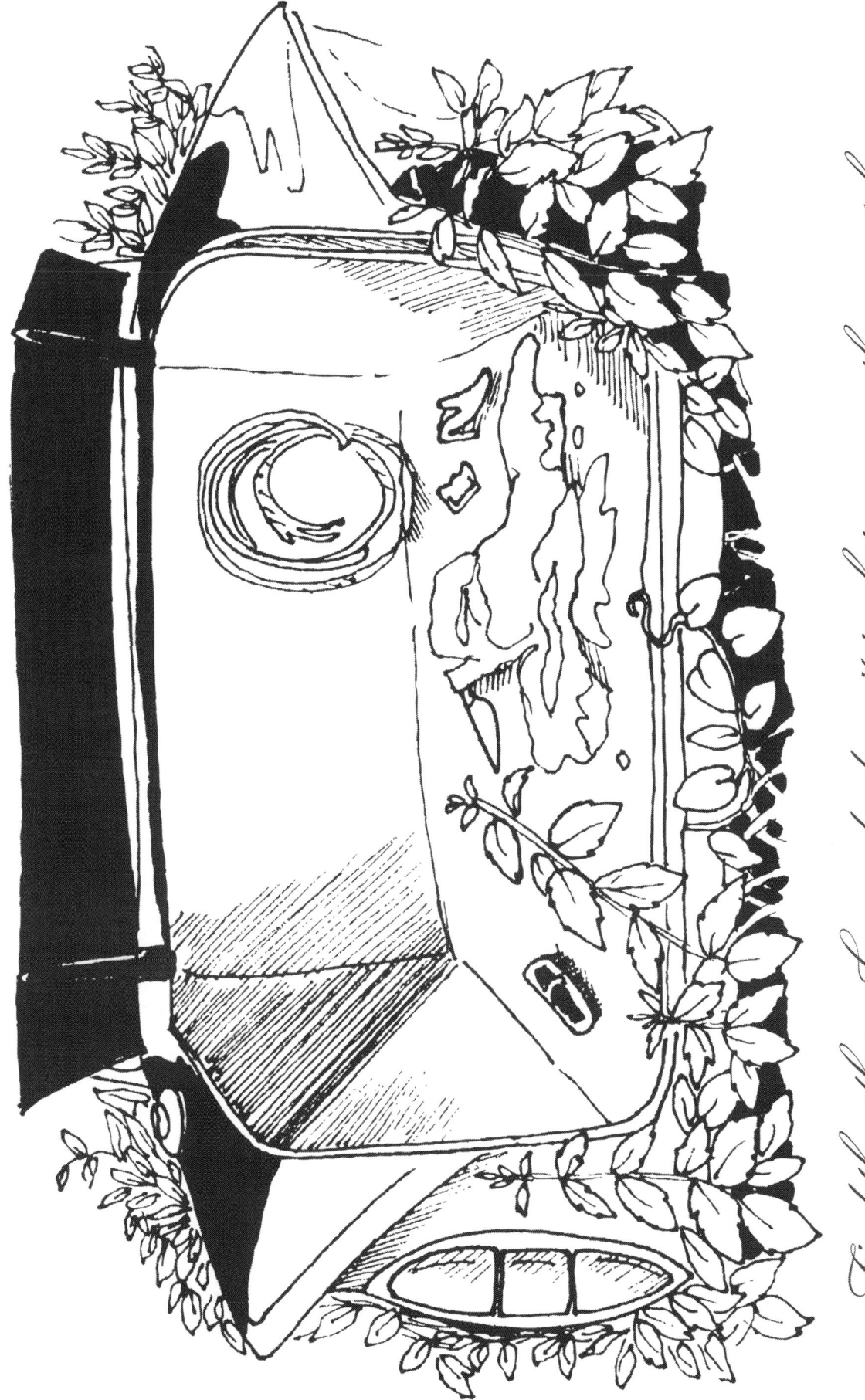

- Find the other shoe and colour it in, being sure they match -

The missing half of the photo from the victim's bag!

I recognised the face immediately — it was the young man from the seed company.

I decided to find out more about the young man and headed the next morning to the neighbour who lived opposite.

She kindly invited me in and sat cuddling her small dog whilst I asked her some questions.

"The young man — is his name Simon?"

She nodded.

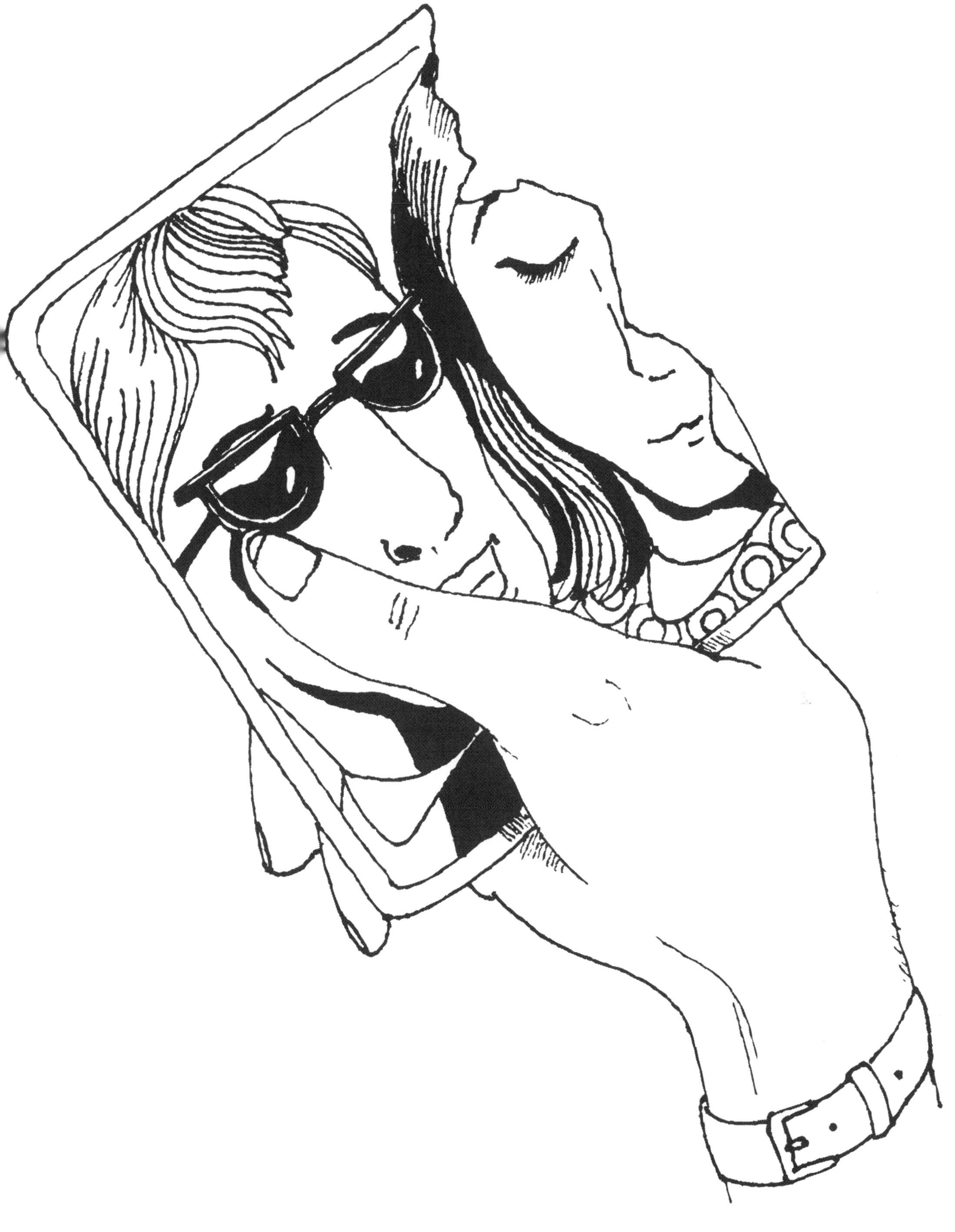

"Have you ever seen a young lady on the premises?"

She explained that a young lady visited often, even more so in the past couple of days. She had heard a commotion one night and saw the two outside.

"It looked as though the young lady was crying." She said.

"Do you know anything about Mr Redtouch?" I asked.

"He's been away a lot on business lately. I know he collects seeds from around the world, so he's away for long periods of time. When he's around, he gets lots of callers to the door – they all look rather scruffy, hippy individuals." She looked slightly disgusted when saying this.

I thanked her and left. Her little dog wagged its tail and tried to follow me

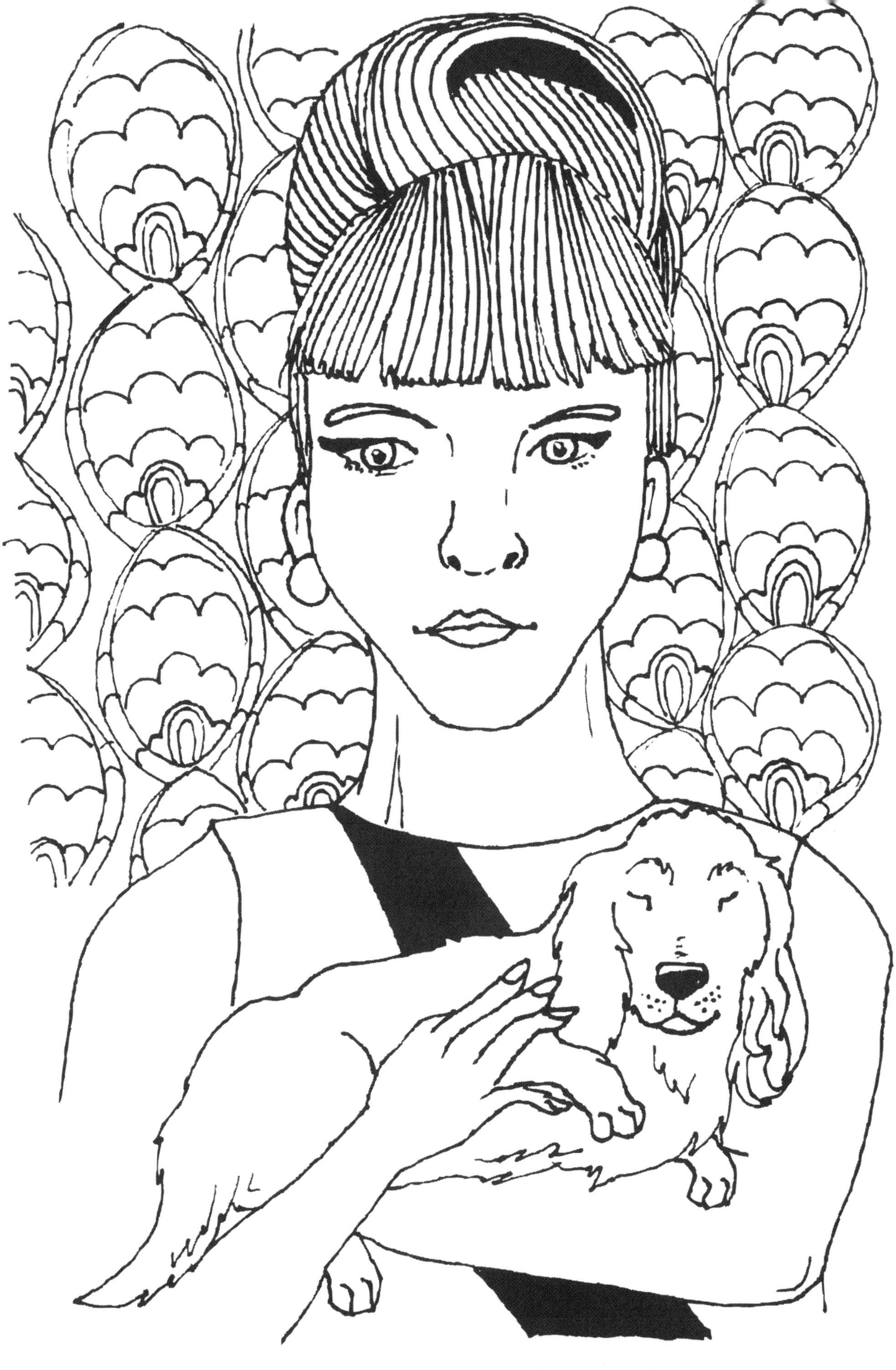

When I returned to my office, there was an urgent call to investigate a body found nearby in the middle of the main village street.

A young man dressed in vibrant colours lay across the concrete.

There was something in his hand. I bent down to take a closer look.

Between his fingers was a rolled cigarette and under his palm rested two seed packets and a receipt from Janma Seed Company.

I pulled the packets out from underneath and sniffed them. I coughed and held it away.

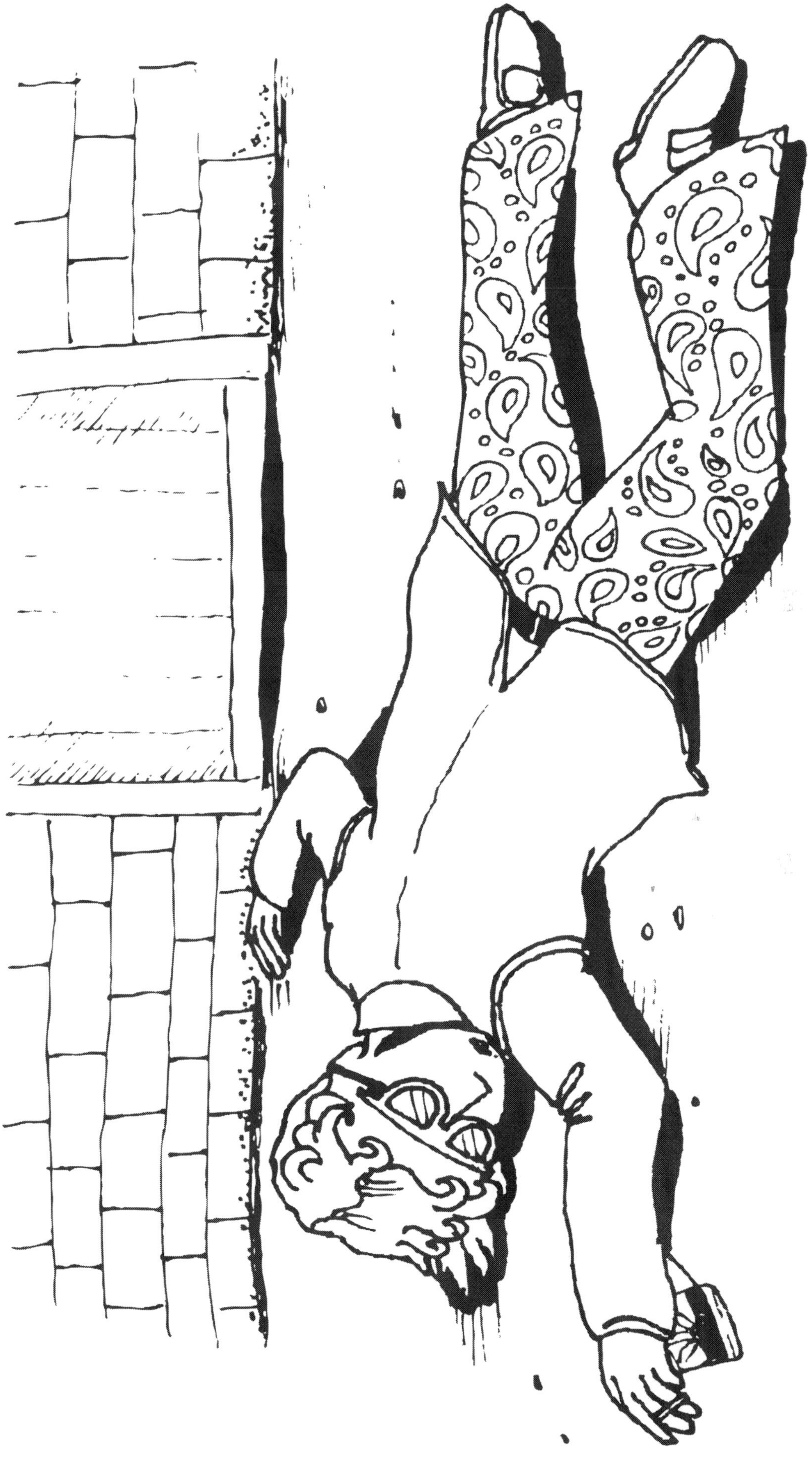

The contents were not seeds, but a fine, silky powder.

It suddenly clicked. The fancy cars. The big house.

Janma Seed Company was using flower seeds as a cover up. Their main customer base was somewhat different. No wonder Mr Redtouch had left in a hurry.

The young girl found in the tree was Simon's girlfriend. He tried to dump her before she found out about the business. She refused to leave him, so he deliberately plotted a public affair with her best friend.

Concerned she still may have known too much, Simon and his new girlfriend plotted to kill his ex.

Foolishly, they tried to cover up the murder by arranging her in a tree and slashing her to look like a leopard attack.

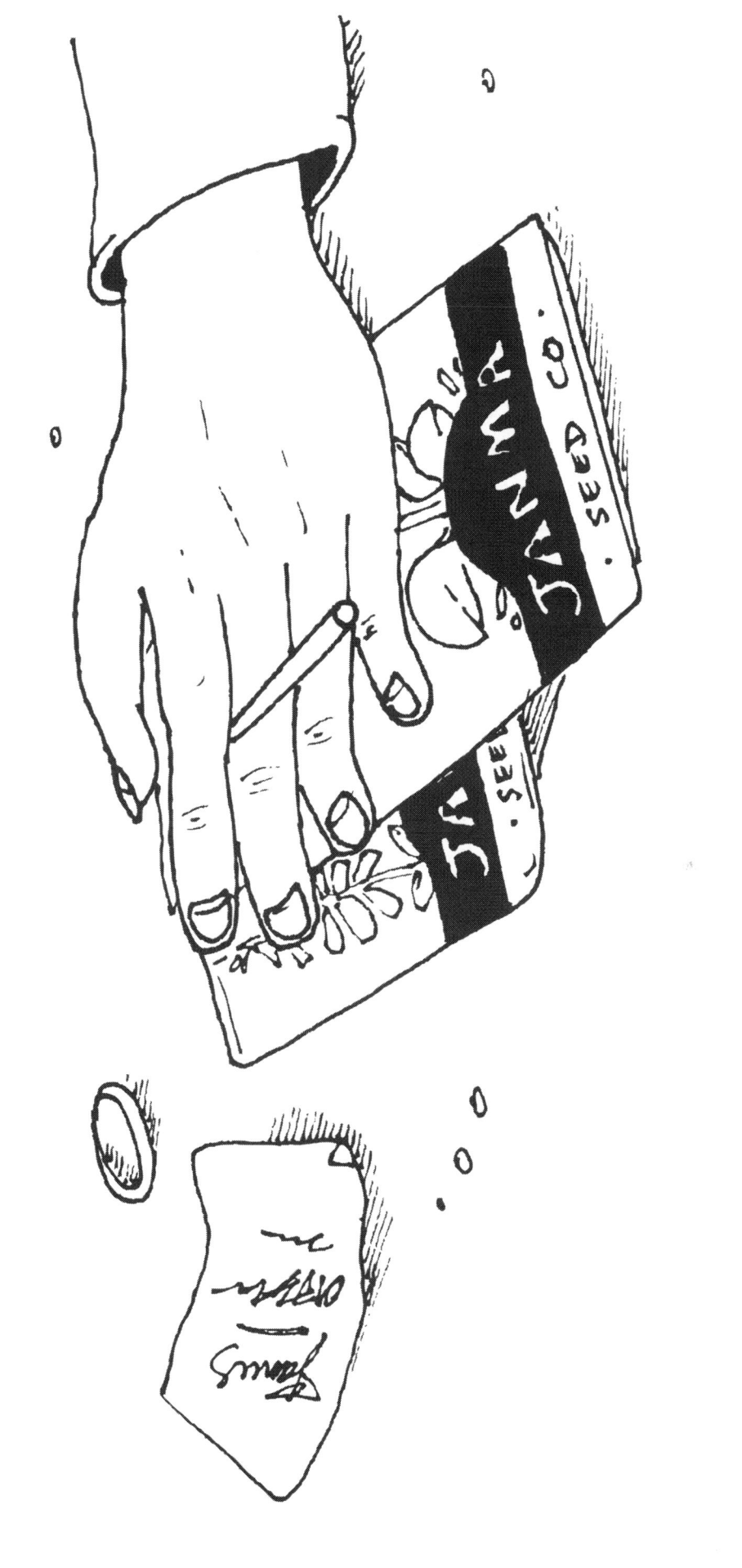

~ Find the other six coins and colour them in ~

I called Sergeant Rowde and explained the case to him, showing him my notes about Janma Seed Company.

"You see here, sir, Janus was two-faced. The name Janma comes from two words and shows Mr Redtouch's love of Latin. 'Jan' comes from Janus and 'ma' comes from the abbreviation of Matutine Pater, a pun of 'morning father,' or 'mourning father', after the loss of his son.

The business is two-faced and the flower seeds are used as a cover for selling items of consumption.

Little did they know that playing a leopard attack would draw more attention to the case."

The Sergeant nodded and I got in the car with him to drive to Janma Seeds.

- Draw some filing cabinets behind Sergeant Rowde -

We knocked on the heavy front door and awaited an answer.

Unsurprisingly, no-one came.

I looked around and spotted a small car parked under a tree at the edge of the driveway. It was the girlfriend's car.

"They're both here."

I tried the handle and the door swung open.

We dashed inside and found the shocked couple standing in the conservatory.

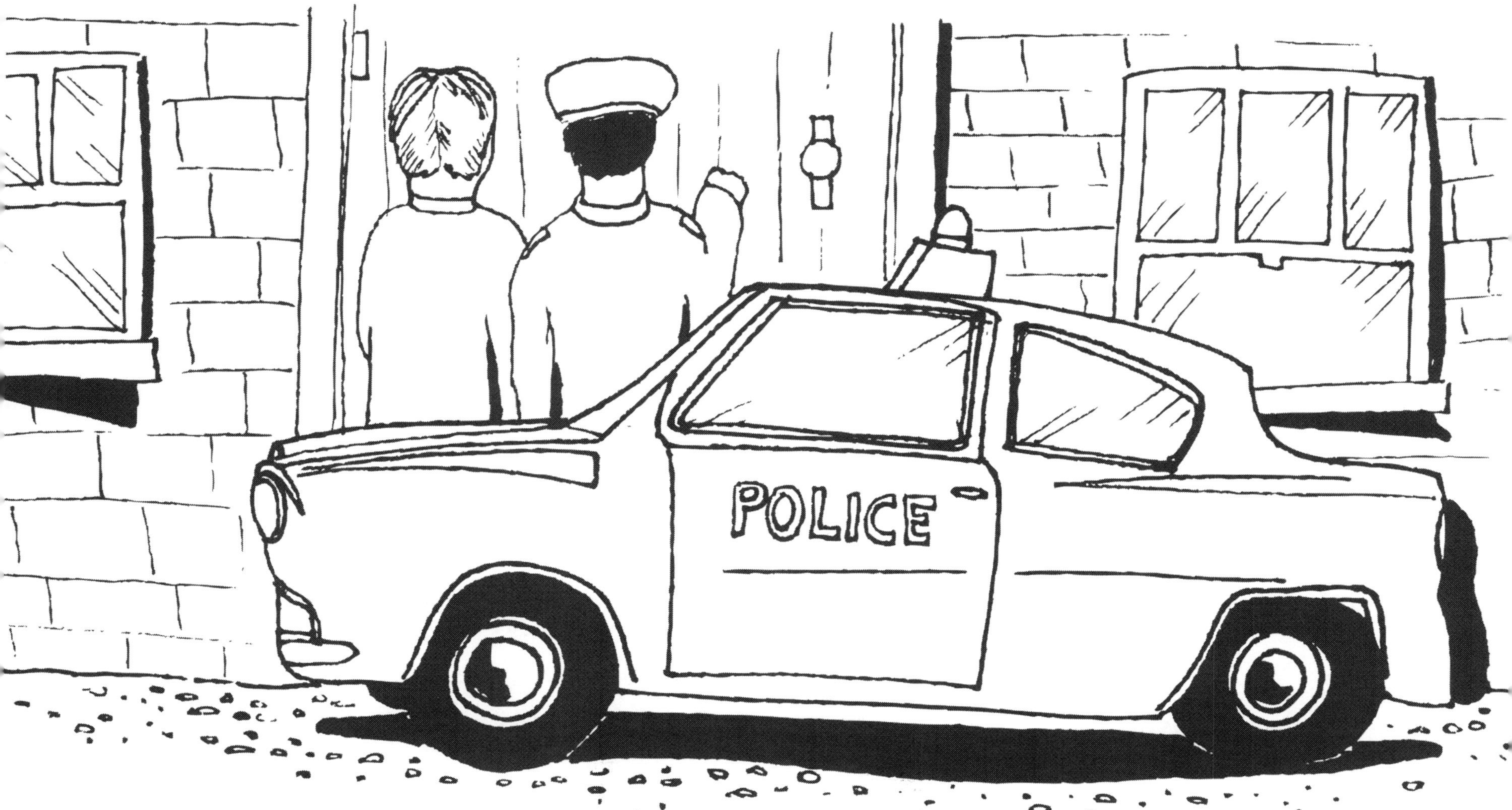
POLICE

"You're under arrest. We think you know why."

The case was solved — all we needed was to catch Mr Redtouch, who could be anywhere in the world right now.

Italy looks favourite. *Fancy a trip?*

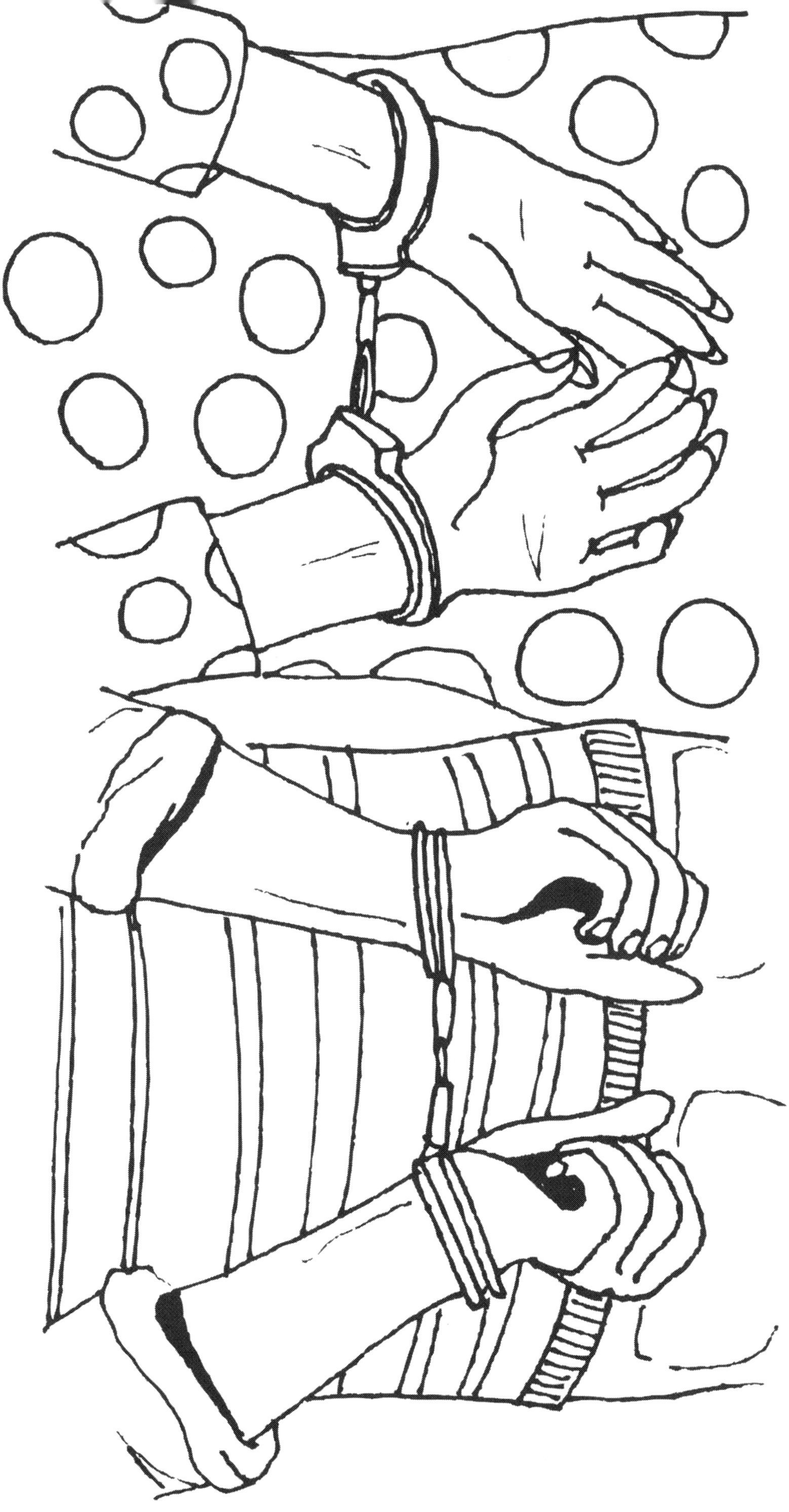

Printed in Great Britain
by Amazon